COLLECTIBLE ACTION FIGURES

SECOND EDITION

Identification & Value Guide

Paris and Susan Manos

COLLECTOR BOOKS
A Division of Schroeder Publishing Co., Inc.

The current values in this book should be used only as a guide. They are not intended to set prices, which vary from one section of the country to another. Auction prices, as well as dealer prices vary greatly and are affected by condition as well as demand. Neither the authors nor the publisher assume responsibility for any losses that might be incurred as a result of consulting this guide.

The prices shown in this guide are derrived by the authors, wholly independent of Hasbro, Ideal, Mego, Kenner, Louis Marx, Gabriel, Matchbox, Gilbert, and Mattel and has no connection therewith.

This book makes reference to G.I. Joe®, Captain Action®, Ken®, and other identities for various figures produced by Hasbro, Ideal, and Mattel, which are trademarks of their respective manufacturers.

Searching For A Publisher?

We are always looking for knowledgeable people considered to be experts within their fields. If you feel that there is a real need for a book on your collectible subject and have a large comprehensive collection, contact Collector Books.

On the Cover:
G.I. Joe Arctic Assault Mission, page 65; Gold Knight and horse by Marx, page 123; Dr. Steel, page 133; Captain America, page 88; Bible Greats, page 151; and Cub Scout, Craig, page 127.

Cover Design: Beth Summers
Book Design: Beth Ray

Additional copies of this book may be ordered from:

Collector Books
P.O. Box 3009
Paducah, Ky 42002-3009

@$17.95. Add $2.00 each for postage and handling.

Copyright © 1996 by Paris and Susan Manos
Updated Values 1998

This book or any part thereof may not be reproduced without the written consent of the Authors and Publisher.

DEDICATION

This book is dedicated to the most important person in our lives.

**Our Loving Daughter
Carol Manos**

Thank you for your help:
Scott Mick
Marianne Ocker
Faith & Dan Wagner

INTRODUCTION

Collectible Male Action Figures

The need for information on collectible male action figures has grown over the past ten years. As male action figures and dolls become more collectible, the quest for information on this subject grows, and the need for qualified written material becomes greater.

No one can say that he is an expert in any segment of the world of collecting, as there is always something new and exciting a collector can discover about an item, no matter how many times it has been written about.

Collectors gather information in their own way. Be it through old store catalogs, magazines, or booklets, as they acquire more knowlege, they share it with other interested hobbyists.

I know for a fact, the more I learn, the more important it becomes to me to share my research facts. I find it gratifying to do this because in doing so, more and more join in on the excitement, and thus, the not too well known treasure gains recognition and becomes an artifact.

For this reason, I have gathered all my research and enthusiasm in this simple picture book "Collectible Male Action Figures."

PRICING GUIDE

Pricing in this book is based on Mint-In-Box (M.I.B.), Mint-In-Package (M.I.P.), Mint-On-Card (M.O.C.) and mint condition items.

Pricing beyond this scale is left to the discretion of the individual.

CONTENTS

Three rare police uniforms. Air Security, M.P. green. $550.00. M.P. tan with black. $550.00. Yellow helmets and radio. $550.00.

CONTENTS

AMERICA'S FIGHTING
MAN FIGURES

From the beginning of time, boys played with toy soldiers. Archaeologists have unearthed small gold warrior figures and dolls from ancient Greek tombs where children were buried.

This manner of play has continued through the centuries. Boys as well as grown men are continually fascinated by war games. Many years ago, in a make-believe atmosphere, young boys would engage in battle with toy (cast metal) soldiers. Today, they play with combat ready, dressed action figures.

These play items through the generations have become highly collectible, not only with men, but with women as well.

This chapter will deal with G.I. Joe® action figures in combat and in adventure, by description and collectible value.

G.I. JOE® IDENTIFICATION MARKINGS & DATES

1964

Action Soldier #7500 in realistic Army fatigues, cap, and brown jump boots. Also, training manual, G. I. Joe® dog tag, and set of insignias. Order catalog included. Assorted hair and eye colors. $275.00.

G.I. JOE® IDENTIFICATION MARKINGS & DATES

1964
Marked on right, lower back:
> G.I. Joe T. M. (Trademark)
> Copyright 1964
> By Hasbro R
> Patent Pending
> Made in U.S.A.

1965
Slight change In marking:
> G.I. Joe R (Registered)
> Copyright 1964
> By Hasbro R
> Patent Pending
> Made In U.S.A.

This mark appears on all four branches of the armed services, excluding the black action figures. All figures have hard plastic heads.

1966
Same markings as 1965:
> French Resistance Fighter
> Japanese Imperial Soldier
> Australian Jungle Fighter
> German Soldier

These figures have hard plastic heads but no facial scars.

1967 – 1968 – 1969
Markings changed:
> G.I. Joe R
> Copyright 1964
> By Hasbro R
> Pat. No. 3,277,602
> Made in U.S.A.

Heads are made of a semi-hard vinyl.
A talking mechanism was added to the line, with the exception of the black figures.

G.I. NURSE®

Marked across back waist:
> Patent Pending R
> 1967 Hasbro
> Made in Hong Kong

Hard plastic jointed body and vinyl head.

1970 – 1975
Markings remained the same:
> G.I. Joe R
> Copyright 1964
> By Hasbro R
> Pat. no. 3,277,602
> Made in U.S.A.

1975 – 1976
Markings changed:
> c 1975 Hasbro R
> Pat. Pend., Pawt. R. I.

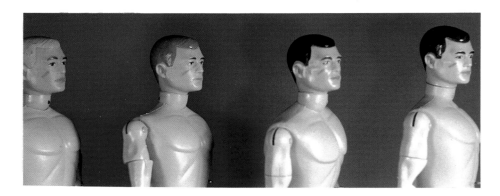

G. I. Joe® action figures came in four haircolors: blond, auburn, black, and brown. Each figure has a scar on the right cheek. These figures were sold in four basic packages: Action Soldier, Action Sailor, Action Marine, and Action Pilot.

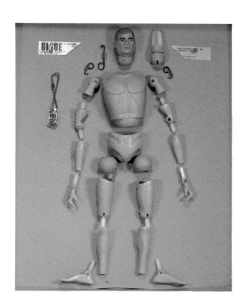

As advertised in 1964, G. I. Joe® has 21 movable parts which enabled him to assume many action positions.

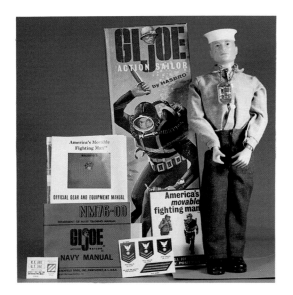

Action Sailor #7600 in light blue denim work shirt, navy blue denim work pants, white Navy cap, and black boots. G.I. Joe® dog tag, Navy training manual, and a set of insignias included. Assorted hair and eye colors. $275.00.

Action Pilot #7800 in orange zippered jumpsuit, black boots, and blue fatigue cap. Also, Air Force training manual, set of insignias, and G.I. Joe® dog tag. Assorted hair and eye colors. $300.00.

Action Marine #7700 in camouflaged fatigue shirt and pants with brown jump boots. Also, G.I. Joe® dog tag, set of insignias, and Marine training manual. Assorted hair and eye colors. $275.00.

Black Action Soldier #7500 in original fatigues. Black Action Soldier re-dressed in Marine camouflaged fatigues. $750.00.

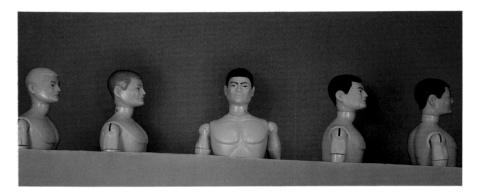

1966 Action Soldiers of the World. Members of this set may have any hair and eye color combination. These figures have no facial scar.

1966 French Resistance Fighter in black turtle-neck sweater, blue denim pants with stitched simulated pockets (unlike sailor fatigue pants), and black vinyl beret. Figure, $400.00; accessories pack, $125.00; figure w/accessories $550.00.

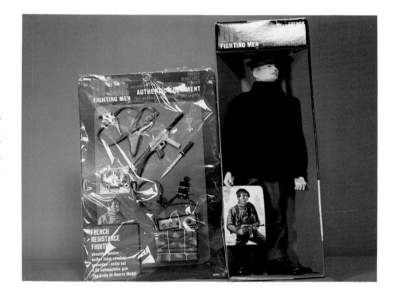

1966 German Soldier. Figure, $350.00; accessories, $125.00; figure and accessories, $550.00.

1966 Japanese Imperial Soldier.
Figure, $475.00;
accessories pack, $150.00;
figure and accessories, $575.00.

1966 British Commando.
Figure, $425.00;
accessories pack, $125.00;
figure and accessories, $475.00.

1966 Russian Infantry Man.
Figure, $425.00;
accessories pack, $125.00;
figure and accessories, $500.00.

GI Joe

1966 British and Canadian Commando. This is a rare and hard-to-find item. This figure was made by Hasbro of Canada. $800.00.

1966 Australian Jungle Fighter. Figure, $375.00; accessories pack, $125.00; figure and accessories, $500.00.

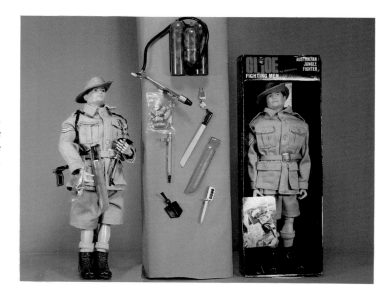

Official membership pack including welcome letter, membership certificate, life-size dog tag, membership card, and iron-on transfer. $100.00 unused.

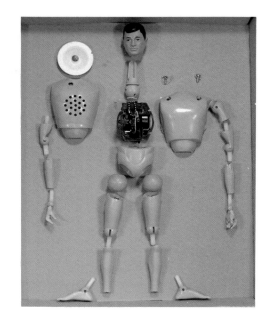

1967 "America's Movable Fighting Man" talks.

1967 Talking Action Soldiers. $300.00.

Talking Action Marine. $350.00.

Talking Action Pilot. $375.00.

Talking Action Sailor (not photographed). $300.00.

1969 Green Beret. Any hair and eye color. Figure, $275.00; figure and accessories, $375.00.

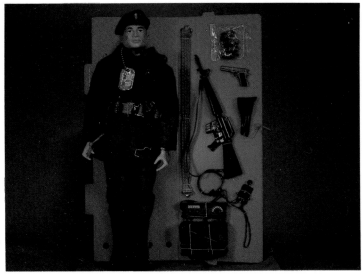

1969 Green Beret.
Figure (out of box), $250.00 to $275.00.
Bazooka pack, $70.00.

1967 G.I. Nurse®. The only female in this action series. Hard plastic jointed body, vinyl head with rooted short ash blonde hair, and blue-green painted eyes. $1,000.00.

1969 Talking Astronaut. $275.00.

1966 Space Capsule Box.

DRESSED FIGURES,
UNIFORMS, AND ACCESSORY PACKS

G.I. Joe® Sailor - Dress Uniform. First uniform mint and complete with dog tag. $175.00.

Talking Sailor - Second uniform mint and complete. $200.00.

First uniform with zipper from waist to sleeve cuff. Second uniform with zipper from waist to armpit.

Combination Navy Attack Set #7607, plus Navy Attack Helmet Set #7610 shown on Action Sailor. $200.00.

Rare Marine Jungle Fighter Set #7732. $350.00.

(1) Arisaka rifle and bayonet (Japanese Soldier). (2) M 1 rifle. (3) 45 caliber automatic machine gun. (4) Russian infantry man machine gun. (5) British commando sten sub-machine gun and clip. (6) M-60 machine gun. (7) White dress rifle. (8) Carbin and bayonet. (9) French resistance fighter 7-65 sub-machine gun. (10) German soldier 9mm Schmeisse pistol. (11) AR-15 rifle. (12) AR-15 jungle fighter rifle. (13) M-16 rifle. (14) 40mm grenade launcher. (15) Machine Gun and tripod (16) 81mm mortar.

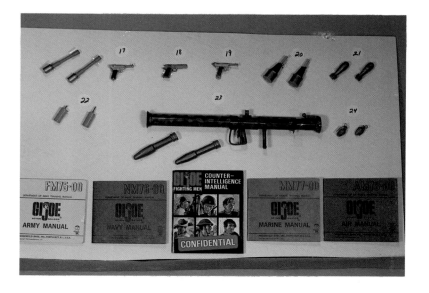

(17) German soldier grenades and Luger pistol. (18) Automatic pistol, cal. 45. (19) Japanese imperial soldier Mamba pistol. (20) Russian anti-tank grenade. (21) Mortar shells. (22) Underwater dynamite. (23) Bazooka and projectiles. (24) Hand grenades.

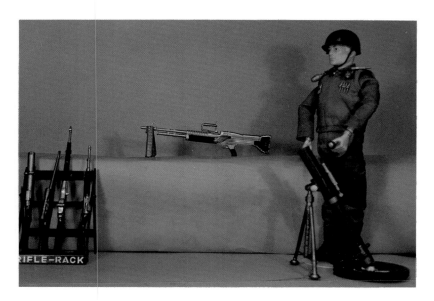

Weapons rack #7727 with M-60 and AR-15 rifles, carbine, and 40mm grenade launcher. $100.00. Heavy Weapons Set #7538. 81mm mortar with 3 shells, M-610 machine gun, bipod, bullet-proof vest with bullets and hand grenades, and 40-round ammunition belt. $275.00 with figure.

Tank Commander Set #7731. Set includes an authentically-styled brown tanker jacket, tanker helmet, machine gun, tripod, ammo box, belt, radio, and tripod. $300.00 with figure.

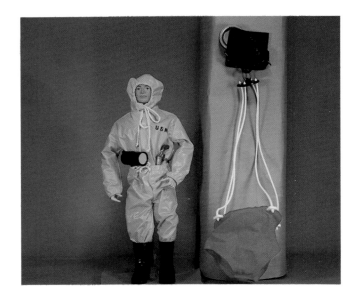

Breeches Buoy #7625. Set includes buoy, slicker jacket and pants, flare gun, blinker light. $325.00 with figure.

Commando Outfit. Set includes raft with anchor and paddle, flare gun, blinker light, black knit stocking cap (hard to find), 45 caliber automatic machine gun, gas mask, wireless with earphone, TNT with detonator, and binoculars. $325.00 with figure.

Communications Flag Set #7704. Flags for Army, Air Corps, Marines, and Navy, plus Old Glory. $125.00.

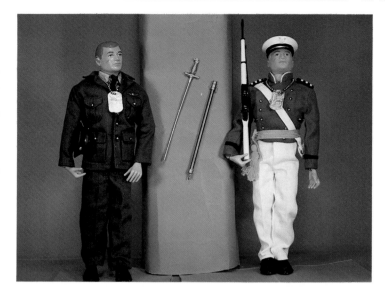

Air Corps Dress Uniform #7803. Authentic dress uniform complete with dress blue jacket and trousers, light blue shirt, tie and garrison cap, plus wings and captain's bars. $250.00 with figure.

Air Cadet #7822. This set came in a photo covered box as well as an open cellophane covered box. (Photo boxed is more desirable.) $275.00 with figure; $575.00 photo boxed; $225.00 celo-covered box.

West Point Cadet #7537. This set came photo boxed as well as in an open celo covered box. (Printed box is more desirable.)
With figure, $300.00;
photo boxed, $325.00;
open front box, $225.00.

Annapolis Cadet #7624. This set came boxed as shown or in an open celo covered box. (Printed box is more desirable.) With figure, $325.00; photo boxed, $325.00; open front box, $225.00.

Action Marine Dress Parade Set #7710. Includes authentically tailored dress jacket with brass buttons, trousers with red stripe sewn to sides, cap, belt, rifle, and Marine manual. $225.00; with figure, $250.00.

Action Marine. Sold through Sears catalog in shipping box. Dressed in Dress Parade Set including dog tag, insignias, and Marine manual. $250.00.

Military Police Set #7521. Authentic Ike jacket with ascot and pants in Army fabric, 45 pistol with holster, arm band, billy club, duffle bag, and Army manual, $300.00. Helmet and accessories pack #7526 (not photographed). $125.00; with figure, $250.00.

Action Sailor "Shore Patrol Set" #7612 (not photographed). Includes dress jumper, pants, 45 pistol, white belt, cap, sea bag, billy stick, arm band, and neckerchief. These pieces also came in small individual packs (as shown). $175.00; with figure, $200.00.

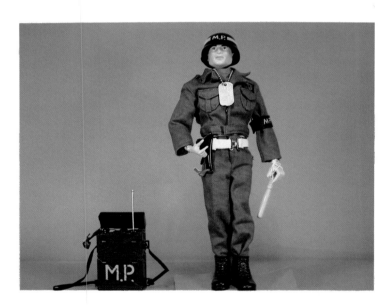

Military Police #7539. Very rare turquoise Ike jacket with airborn emblem over left pocket, trousers, 45 pistol with holster, billy club, belt, black and gold helmet, radio, and arm band. This same set came in a light beige color as well and is equally as hard to find. $550.00.

Action Marine Medic Set #7719. Includes stretcher, first-aid shoulder pouch, stethoscope, plasma bottle, bandages, red cross flag, splints, crutch, and arm bands. Set, $175.00; individual packs, $100.00; with figure, $225.00.

Action figures back from combat, Medic and accessories. $225.00.

Action Marine (as shown). $100.00.

Action Pilot Set #7823. This set comes with an actual working parachute and pack, Mae-West life jacket, G-suit, crash helmet has face mask, hose connection, and tinted visor. Also included are flight coveralls, boots, and flashlight. $225.00; with figure, $275.00.

Action Pilot Scramble Set #7807. Includes authentic zippered flight suit, air vest, pistol belt with 45 and holster, and clip board with pad and pencil. $175.00.

Small pack Scramble Crash Helmet #7810. $50.00.

Parachute pack #7811. $45.00.
With figure, $200.00.

Test Pilot Outfit also referred to as "Fantastic Freefall" from the adventures of G.I. Joe®. Set includes, boots, orange coveralls, gold pilots helmet, Mae-West life vest, flashlight, working parachute and case, and blinker light. $250.00.

Deck Commander Set #7621. Includes safety striped jump suit, cloth helmet with earphones, signal paddles, clip board with pad and pencil, binoculars, and flare gun.
Set, $150.00; pack set, $125.00; with figure, $225.00.

Deep Sea Diver Set #7620. This set contains a waterproof suit, helmet with face mask that opens and closes, air pump with 24" long hoses, weighted belt, shoes, signal float, and deep sea hammer. $125.00; with figure, $175.00.

Astronaut Suit and Space Capsule. Actually designed from "Mercury Control" blue prints. Set includes a space suit made of fabric used by the real U.S. Astronauts. This set was used twice. First capsule has a blue interior, the second issue has a white interior. $125.00; dressed figure, $175.00.

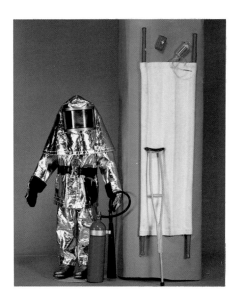

Combat Engineer #7511. Set includes engineer transit and tripod, helmet, and 45mm automatic machine gun. $250.00.

Combat Construction Set #7572 includes jack hammer, construction helmet, and gray work gloves. Pack set, $150.00; with figure, $200.00.

Fire Fighter Rescue Set. Includes real metallic heat suit with protective hood, gloves, boots, belt with handy accessories, chemical spray tank with nozzle, stretcher, first-aid kit, plasma bottle, and crutch. $300.00 dressed figure with accessories.

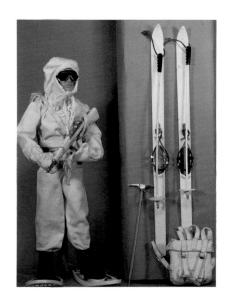

Mountain Troops Set #7530. Includes winter white camouflage pack, web belt, snowshoes, ice axe, climbing ropes, and grenades. $125.00.

Ski Patrol Set #7531. Includes winter white camouflage, two-piece ski parka, boots, goggles, mittens, skis, and poles. $175.00; with figure, $200.00.

Frogman Underwater Demolition Set #7602. Includes rubber suit, headpiece, face mask, swim fins, scuba tank, knife, scabbard, depth gauge, and dynamite. $175.00 set; individual pack pieces, $75.00; dressed figure, $200.00.

Deep Freeze Set. Includes fur parka, ski pants, ice boots, snow sled with tow rope, flare gun, and ice pick. $250.00.

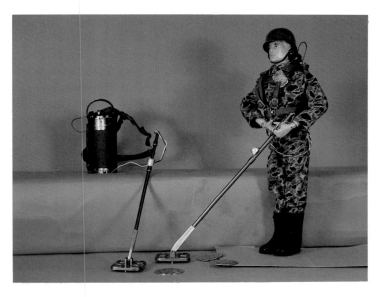

Demolition Set. Includes mine detector, power pack, earphones, and mines. $150.00; dressed figure, $200.00.

These outfits were not distributed to all areas. They were packaged in plastic baggies. These outfits were very well made.

Police Officer. $225.00.

Race Car Driver. $150.00.

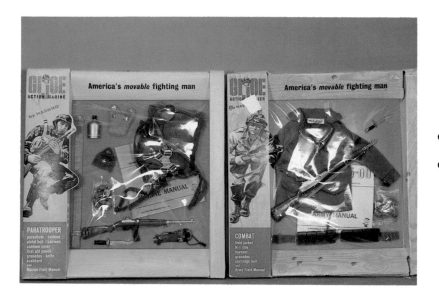

Combat Field Pack #7502. $100.00.

Combat Field Jacket Set #7501. $100.00.

Action Soldier-Bivouac Deluxe Pup Tent Set #7513. $175.00.

Action Marine-Communications Post Poncho Set #7701. $175.00.

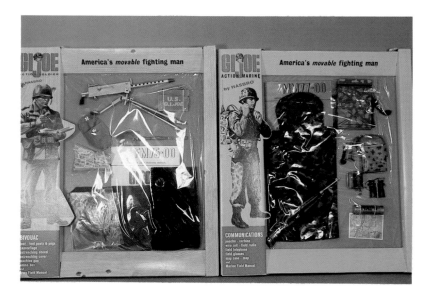

Military Police Set #7521. $175.00.

Marine Dress Parade Set #7710. $175.00.

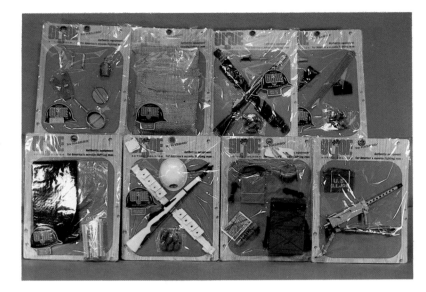

Assorted G.I. Joe® - Action Soldier Packs. $50.00 to $75.00 each.

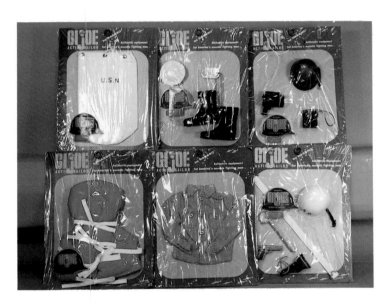

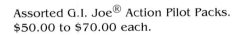

Assorted G.I. Joe® Action Sailor Packs. $50.00 to $70.00 each.

Assorted G.I. Joe® Action Pilot Packs. $50.00 to $70.00 each.

G.I. Joe® Assorted Action Sailor Packs.
$55.00 to $75.00 each.

G.I. Joe® Action Soldier Bazooka
Packs. $100.00.

Green Beret Pack. $125.00.
All others $50.00 to $70.00 each.

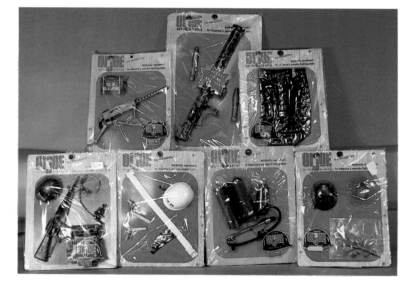

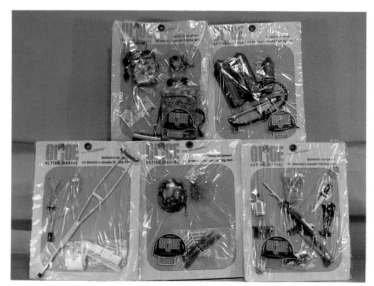

Assorted G.I. Joe® Action Marine Packs.
$50.00 to $70.00 each.

Special Offer: 4 Services in 1 Special. Accessories varied in count from 12 to 14 to 16 pieces, loose in plastic bag. Each set came with a 4 in 1 comic book.

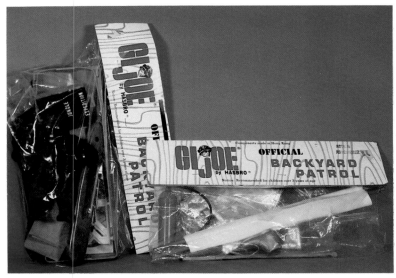

Backyard Patrol Pack Sets.

Adventure Team Set. $75.00.

Crash Crew Set. $150.00.

Backyard Patrol Pack Sets.

Astronaut Suit Astronaut Accessories Pack. $75.00.

Adventure Team Play Set. $75.00.

Astronaut Suit with Mine Sweeper. $150.00.

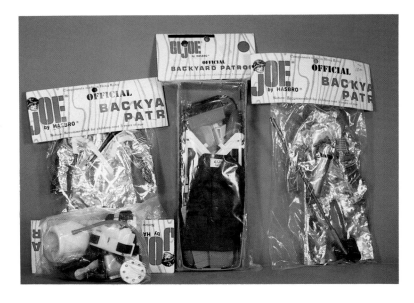

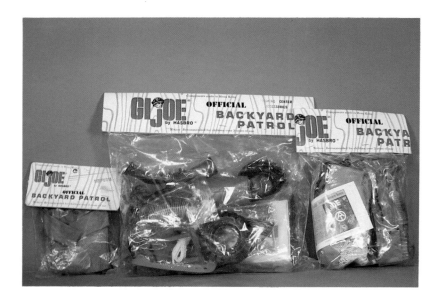

Backyard Patrol Japanese Soldier Suit and Helmet. $50.00.

Field Accessory Pack. $75.00.

Adventure Team Play Set. $65.00.

The Adventures of G.I. Joe® Underwater Diver Play Set. The Eight Ropes of Danger. $200.00.

The Adventures of G.I. Joe® Jungle Explorer. Figure included. The Mouth of Doom. $275.00.

The Adventures of G.I. Joe®
Spaceman Play Set. Hidden Missile
Discovery. $200.00.

The Adventures Of G.I. Joe® Polar Explorer.
Figure included. The Fight For Survival.
$325.00.

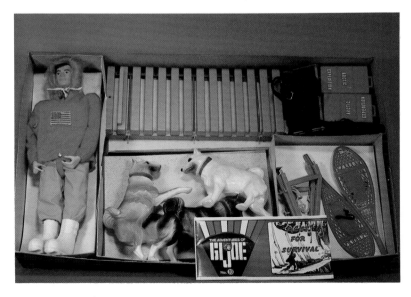

The Adventures of G.I. Joe® Sea Adventure. Figure included. The Shark's Surprise. $275.00.

The Adventures of G.I. Joe® Astronaut Hidden Missile Discovery. $225.00.

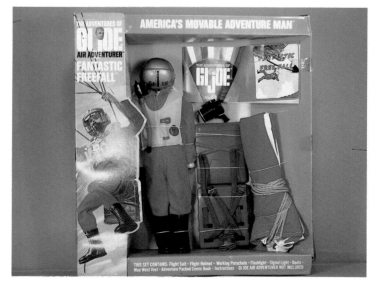

The Adventures of G.I. Joe® Air Adventure Fantastic Freefall. $225.00.

ADVENTURE TEAM ERA
1970–1976

Adventure Team Membership Kit. Includes: Welcome letter, certificate of membership, dog tag, iron-on transfer, and membership I.D. card (not shown). $50.00.

The G.I. Joe® Adventure Team. Top Left: Black Adventurer. Top Right: Air Adventurer. Bottom: Left to Right, Talking Astronaut, Sea Adventurer, Talking Team Commander, Land Adventurer.

G.I. Joe® Man of Action with insignias and dog tag like Action Soldier but Adventure Team Emblem on shirt. $175.00.

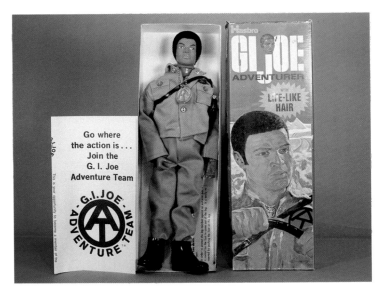

Black Adventurer. $225.00.

Talking Adventurer Team Commander. $200.00.

Land Adventurer. $175.00.

Sea Adventurer. $175.00.

Air Adventurer. $175.00.

Talking Man of Action. $200.00.

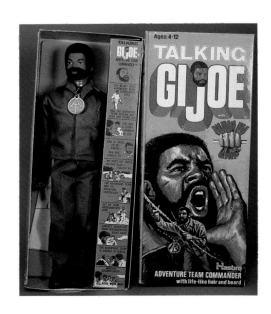

Black Talking G.I. Joe® with Kung Fu Grip. $225.00.

Adventure Team G.I. Joe® with Kung Fu Grip. $175.00.

Adventure Team G.I. Joe® with Kung Fu Grip. $175.00.

Adventure Team. G.I. Joe® Black Adventurer with Kung-Fu Grip. $125.00.

Eagle Eye G.I. Joe®, Land Commander. $100.00.

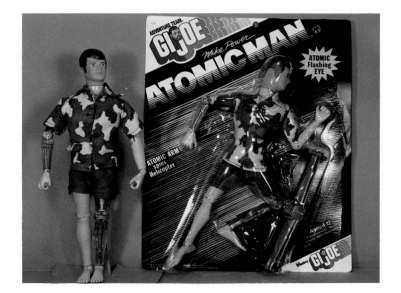

Adventure Team Mike Power Atomic Man.
$100.00; $50.00 out of packaging.

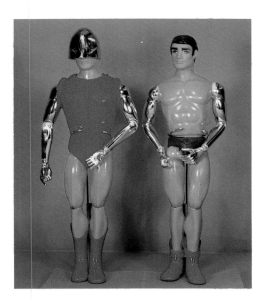

Bullet Man. $85.00.

1977 Super Joe - 8¾" tall. $35.00. Made
between 11½" G.I. Joe® figure and 3½" figure.

Super Joe. $50.00.

Super Joe Command Center. $45.00.

Assorted Super Joe Play Sets. $35.00 each.

Outfits. $20.00 each.

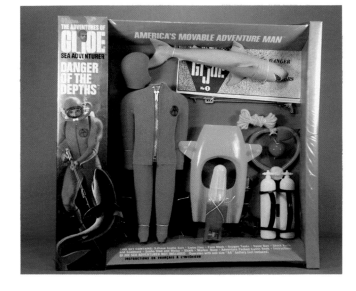

The Adventures of G.I. Joe® Sea Adventure. Danger of the Depths. $200.00.

The Adventures of G.I. Joe®, Land Adventures. White Tiger Hunt. $200.00.

1990 G.I. Joe Collector's Convention (souvenir) in Omaha, hosted by Faith and Dan Wagner.

S.A.C. Honor Guard. $300.00.

Navy Dress Whites. $125.00.

Infantry Uniform (pictured), 1993 Navy Dress Whites. $125.00.
Hosted by James De Simone in California.

Not shown 1992 G.I. Joe Collector's Club Convention. $125.00.

1994 International G.I. Joe Collector's Convention in New York sponsored by Marz Productions and Hasbro.

Action Pilot. $550.00.

Military Police. $650.00.

1994 Commemorative (Green Beret Figure) mail-in offer by Hasbro. $400.00.

Prototype head sculpture used to salute 30th commemorative 12" figures. Autographed by the creators Ken Ellis and Kurt Groem. No price.

Prototype body. Model for hall-of-fame collection. No price.

COMBAT AND ADVENTURE TEAM VEHICLES

Friction-powered Armored Car. 20" long. $125.00.

G.I. Joe® Motorcycle and Side Car, by Irwin For Hasbro. $150.00.

Desert Patrol Jeep #8030. With 50 cal. machine gun. This vehicle came with a driver in desert campaign hat and uniform, boots, and 45 pistol. $200.00.

G.I. Joe® 5 Star Jeep #7000. With working 106 mm recoilless rifle, trailer and tripod, mounted searchlight, and four 106mm projectiles. $200.00.

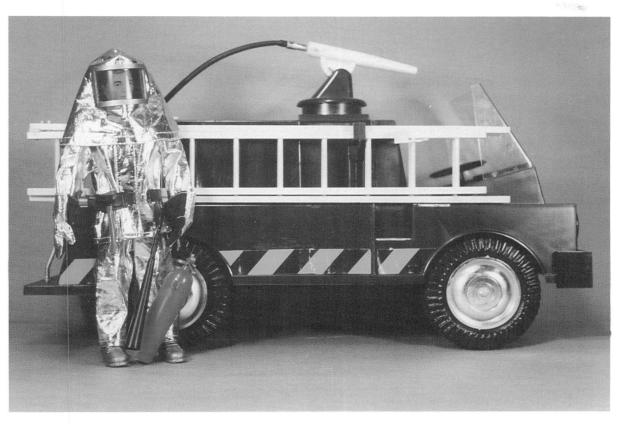

Above: G.I. Joe Crash Crew Truck. $550.00. G.I. Joe Firefighter. $300.00.
Below: Blue Panther Jet, very hard to find. $600.00 mint and complete.

Above: Original box showing jeep and trailer.
Below: G.I. Joe® Official Sea Sled and Frogman. $200.00.

G.I. Joe®, rare official Sea Sled and Cave, Frogman included. This set was a Sears exclusive.
Sets sold elsewhere do not offer the cave. $200.00.

The Adventures of G.I. Joe® Astronaut and Space Capsule. This is the second set. Space Capsule has white interior. $225.00.

First set had dark blue interior. First set was offered by Sears and had a yellow colored flotation collar and raft included. $250.00; flotation collar, $125.00.

This set is very rare and hard to find.

Other vehicles not pictured.

G.I. Amphibian Duck. $300.00.

G.I. Jet Helicopter. $300.00.

G.I. Carrier/Mine Sweeper. This has a long tank and mine sweeper attachment. $250.00.

Jeep, part of J.C. Penney's Exclusive G.I. Joe® Patrol Set. $125.00.

Complete set, includes raft, tent, and gear. $250.00.

Adventure Team Vehicle, rides on land, floats in water. From the Recovery of the Lost Mummy Set. $225.00.

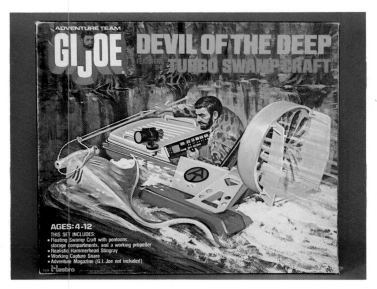

Adventure Team Turbo Swamp Craft. $175.00.

Adventure Team Escape Car. $35.00.

Above: Adventure Team All-Terrain Vehicle Play Set. $125.00.
Below: Adventure Team Helicopter, from The Secret of the Stolen Idol. $100.00.

Above: Adventure Team Sea Wolf. $100.00.
Below: Adventure Team Big Trapper Vehicle, $60.00. Not pictured, G.I. Joe® Mobile Support Unit. $100.00.

COMBAT AND ADVENTURE TEAM
CASES AND TOYS

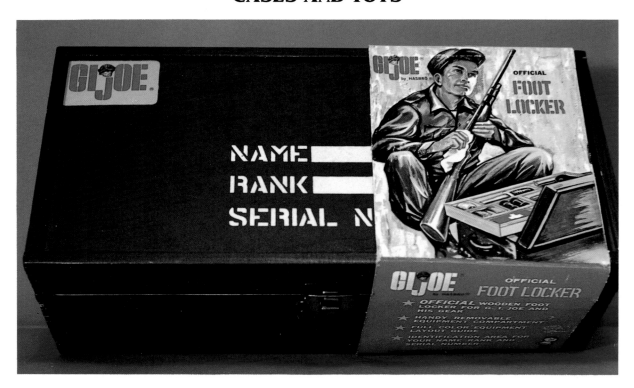

First G.I. Joe® Official Foot Locker and Interior. $60.00.

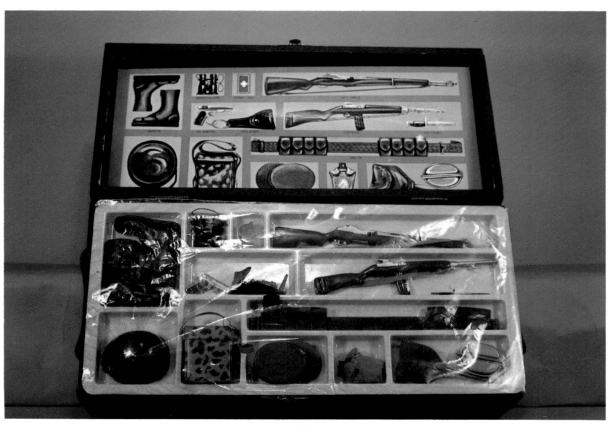

G.I. Joe® Pencil Box by Hasbro. $30.00.

G.I. Joe® Jigsaw Puzzle. $10.00.

Mess Kit. $15.00.

Rare G.I. Joe® Watch, made by Gilbert.
With compass and sighting lenses. $185.00.

Child-size G.I. Joe® Waterproof Poncho and Hood. $45.00.

G.I. Joe® Bop Bag Punching Toy German Soldier, 51" high. $75.00.

G.I. Joe® Adventure Team Colorform Set. $15.00.

G.I. Joe® Adventure Team Dangerous Assignment Game. $20.00.

G.I. Joe® Adventure Team small book and record set. $15.00.

Large book and record. $20.00.

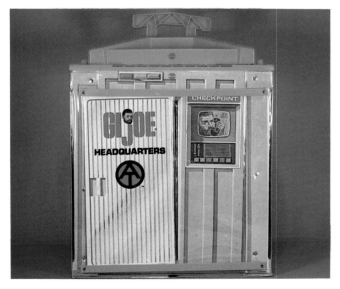

G.I. Joe® Adventure Team Headquarters. $70.00.

Not pictured, Mike Powers Outpost Headquarters. $45.00.

G.I. JOE REISSUED

1991 Duke. First of the series re-issue of the 12"
figure, sold only at Target stores. Red box
interior. $55.00.

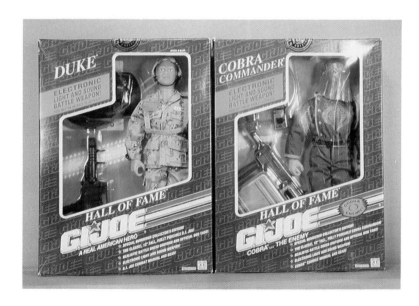

1991 Duke. 2nd issue. Sold throughtout U.S. Box interior a lighter red
than first Duke. $35.00

1991 Cobra Commander. $40.00.

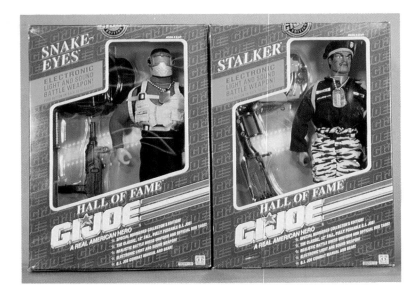

Hall of Fame 1991

Snake Eyes and Stalker. $45.00 ea.

Hall of Fame 1992

Gung Ho. First issue had a gold sword. $55.00.

Second issue had a silver sword. $45.00.

Hall of fame 1992

Storm Shadow. $40.00.

Destro (Cobra Enemy). $40.00.

1964–1994

G.I. Joe® Commemorative
Action Sailor Gift Set. $100.00.

1964–1994

G.I. Joe® Commemorative
Action Marine Gift Set. $100.00.

1964–1994

G.I. Joe® Commemorative
Action Soldier Gift Set (white).
$100.00.

1964 – 1994

G.I. Joe® Commemorative Action Sailor Gift Set. $125.00.

Black soldier hardest to find.

1964 – 1994

Special Issue
Original Action Team in small figures. A real super set, possibly the last of the small figures produced. $75.00.

1993 Hall of Fame

Ultimate Arsenal with authentically styled weapons and gear set. $25.00.

1993 G.I. Joe®

Mobile Artillery Assault Set. $15.00.

Foot Locker. $15.00.

1993 G.I. Joe®

Rhino G.P.V. $50.00.

1993 Hall of Fame

G.I. Joe® Navy Seal Commando
Deluxe Mission Gear. $25.00.

1991 Hall of Fame

G.I. Joe® Strike Cycle. $45.00.

1994 Hall of Fame

G.I. Joe® Cobra Helicopter Attack Set. $45.00.

Schildkrot of Germany - Action Team, Action Girl Underwater Adventure Outfit. $65.00.

Schildkrot of Germany - Action Team, Action Girl Safari Outfit. $65.00.

Not pictured, Action Girl Parachute Adventure. $65.00.

Schildkrot of Germany - Action Team Fire Fighter. $65.00.

Schildkrot of Germany - Action Team Polar Adventure. $65.00.

Schildkrot of Germany - Action Team Medic. $65.00.

Schildkrot of Germany - Action Team Wilderness Adventure. $65.00.

Schildkrot of Germany - Action Team Highway Police. $65.00.

Palitoy of England - Basic Action Man Figure. $95.00.

Palitoy of England - Action Man Soldier and Talking Commander. $125.00 each.

Palitoy of England - Action Man Helicopter Pilot. $125.00.

Palitoy of England - Action Man Space Ranger Talking Commander. $125.00.

Palitoy of England - Action Man Soldier. $95.00.
Accessory pack. $35.00.

Palitoy of England - Action Man Space
Ranger Captain, cloth suit. $150.00.

Palitoy of England - Action Man Space Ranger
Captain, rubber suit. $175.00.

Palitoy of England - Action Man Space Ranger Space
Pirate. $200.00.

Palitoy of England - Action Man
Mounted Police. $150.00.
Dog, $25.00.

Palitoy of England - Action Man. Action Soldier Engineer Pack. $75.00. Action Man Indian
Brave. $100.00.

Tsukuda Japan - Action Man. U.S. Marine Corps, German Trooper, U.S. Army Green Beret. $125.00 each.

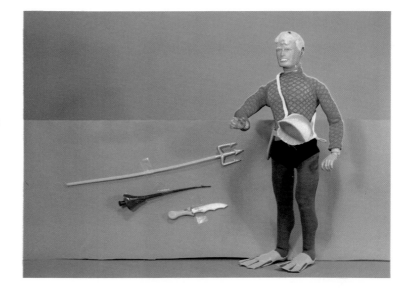

Captain Action® Figure (1966) in Aquaman disguise. $200.00.

Robin. $275.00 mint and complete on figure.

Batman disguise on figure, $275.00 mint and complete.

Dr. Evel. $225.00 mint and complete.

Dr. Evel accessories. $275.00 mint and complete.

Captain Action Flash Gordon. Outfit and accesories only. $150.00 mint and complete.

Batman. Outfit and accessories only. $150.00 mint and complete.

Action Boy® figure (not pictured) 1967, 9" tall. Came in outfit same as Captain Action® figure and accessorized with knife, boomerang, utility belt, beret, and boots. His pet panther was a part of his original outfit. Mint and complete. Bits of original outfit plus pet panther pictured. Panther $50.00.

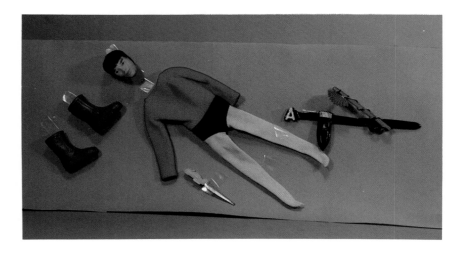

1967 Aqua Lad Disguise, missing spear. $110.00 as is.

KEN® DOLL AND FRIENDS "EVERYDAY LIFE"

Ken® Doll is a male fashion model produced by Mattel Inc. and introduced in 1961 as Barbie® Doll's friend.

Though he may have taken the sideline to make way for the ever-popular Barbie® Doll, Ken® Doll has made a mark of his own in the fashion world.

Ken® Doll represents the all-American boy, a young man that has had a college education and worked in almost every field from fountain boy to astronaut. He is best known, however, as a male fashion model, who along with his friends has been very successful over the years.

This chapter will feature Ken® and Friends Fashion Models, complete wardrobes, and accessories.

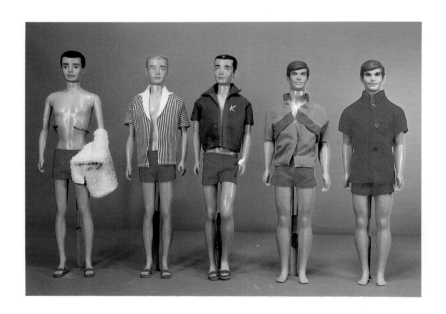

Ken® Doll
1961 – $150.00.
1962 – $100.00.
1964 – $225.00.
1969 – $100.00.

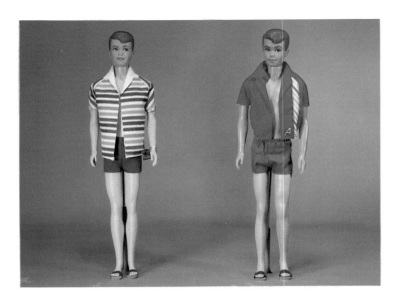

Allen® Doll
1963 – $75.00.
1964 – $225.00.

Talking Brad® Doll (1969). $85.00.

Bendable Ken® (1971). $80.00.

Bendable Brad® (1971). $80.00.

Live Action Ken® Doll on Stage (1971). $90.00.

Walk Lively Ken® Doll (1970). $90.00.

Busy Ken® Doll (1972). $125.00.

Busy Talking Ken® Doll (1972). $175.00.

Mod Hair Ken® Doll (1973). $75.00.

Now Look Ken® Doll (1973). $75.00.

Ken® Tuxedo #787 - Jacket, trousers, dress shirt, black socks and shoes, maroon bow tie and cumberbund, and white rose corsage. $100.00.

Sport Shorts #783 - Sport shirt, Bermuda shorts, khaki socks, and brown oxford shoes. $45.00.

Campus Hero #770 - Sweater, white duck pants, red socks, white oxford shoes, "U" letter, and banner. $50.00.

Ken® Doll in Dreamboat #785 - Sport shirt and jacket, slacks, matching socks, black oxford shoes, and straw hat. $70.00.

Ken® Doll in Casuals #782 - Red sport hat, knit t-shirt, polished cotton pants, striped socks, 2-toned shoes, and key chain and key. $35.00.

Ken® Doll in Saturday Date #786 - Gray suit, long sleeve shirt, striped tie, black shoes and socks. $45.00.

Ken® Doll in Terry Togs #784 - Terry robe, terry scuffs, soap, sponge, terry towel and wash cloth, knit briefs, electric shaver, and comb. $45.00.

Allen® Doll Sleeper Set #781 - Striped P.J.'s, alarm clock, sugarbun, and glass of milk. $30.00.

Ken® Doll "In Training" #780 - Knit t-shirt and briefs, boxer shorts, exercise manual, and dumbell set. $30.00.

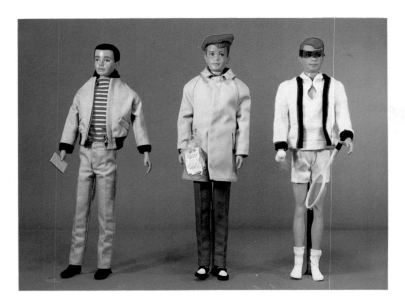

Ken® in "The Yachtsman" #789 - Denim sailing outfit, red striped t-shirt, black shoes, white socks, and yachtsman book. $40.00.

Allen® in "Rally Day" #788 - Tailored beige poplin all-weather coat, red hat, map, and car keys (Slacks and shoes not included). $45.00.

Ken® in "Time For Tennis" #790 - White cardigan, white sport shorts and t-shirt, tennis shoes, socks, goggles, racquet, and ball. $40.00.

Allen® in "Fun On Ice" #791 - Sweater, corduroy slacks, gold socks, cap, mittens, muffler, and racing skates. $50.00.

Ken® in "Army and Airforce" #797 - Armed forces uniform with interchangeable accessories, beige cap, tie, belt, and socks, brown shoes. Also air wings, blue cap, tie and belt, black shoes and socks. $100.00 each.

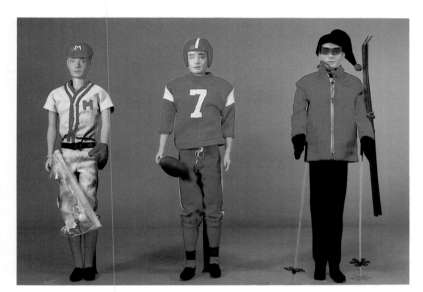

Ken® Doll in "Play Ball" #792 - 2 pc. baseball uniform, regulation shoes, red socks, plastic hat, bat, ball, and mitt. $55.00.

Ken® Doll in "Touchdown" #799 - Red football trousers and sweatshirt, red plastic shoulder guards, football helmet, socks, regulation shoes and socks, and football. $55.00.

Ken® Doll in "Ski Champion" #798 - Red quilted jacket, knitted ski pants, stocking cap, mittens, ski boots, skis, ski poles, and glasses. $65.00.

Ken® Doll in "Red Riding Hood Wolf" #0880 - Checked cap, wolf mask, granny's nightcap. This is part of the set. $70.00.

Ken® Doll in "Arabian Knights" #0774 - Red velvet coat, gold and white sash, gold turban, gold slacks, red velvet scuffs. $125.00.

Ken® Doll in "Masquerade" #794 - Clown costume, mask, scull cap, clown hat, shoes, and invitation. $45.00.

Ken® Doll "Sailor" #796 - Authentic sailor suit and tie, gob cap, duffle bag, socks, and black shoes. $45.00.

Ken® Doll in "Dr. Ken" #793 - Doctor top and trousers, white shoes and socks, doctor bag, surgeons mask and cap, stethescope, and reflector head band. $50.00.

Ken® Doll in "Graduation" #795 - Traditional black gown and mortar board and diploma. $40.00.

Ken® Doll in "King Arthur" #0773 - Silver costume with red satin surcoat with gold belt, scabbard, sword, spurs, helmet, and shield. $125.00.

Ken® Doll in "The Prince" #0772 - Green and gold brocade jacket, white lace collar, velvet and gold knit tights, velvet cape, green velvet shoes, gold velvet cap, velvet pillow with glass slipper. $100.00.

Allen® Doll in "Ken in Switzerland" #0776 - Gray shorts, red suspenders, white shirt, alpine hat, white knee socks, black boots, beer mug, and pipe. $125.00.

Ken® Doll in "Ken in Holland" #0777 - White long sleeved shirt, blue trousers, white knee socks, wooden shoes, blue cap, red paint kerchief, and tulips. $95.00.

Ken® Doll in "Ken in Hawaii" #1404 - Blue and white malu, yellow lei, sandals, straw hat, and ukelele. $80.00.

Ken® Doll in "Ken in Mexico" #1404 - Brown coat and trousers, green cumberbund, white shirt, black bow tie, black boots, and sombrero. $100.00.

Ken® Doll in "Campus Corduroys" #1410 - Beige corduroy jacket and trousers, white shirt, and red tie, $65.00. Pack set, $35.00.

Ken® Doll in "American Airlines Captain" #0779 - Authentic blue suit, captain's cap, black socks and shoes, white shirt, blue tie, flight log, and duffel bag. $100.00.

Ken® Doll in "Campus Hero" #0770 - Same as #0770 (pictured on page 97) only with a letter "M" instead of the letter "U" Same value. $55.00.

Allen® Doll in "Fountain Boy" #1407 - White jacket, white cap, tray with sodas, napkins, spoons, order book, and two pencils. $45.00.

Allen® Doll in "Roller Skate Date" #1405 - Argyle sweater, stocking cap, brown roller skates. Trousers not included in set. $45.00.

Ken® Doll in "Victory Dance" #1411 - Blue blazer, white slacks, red vest, white shirt with red tie, red socks, black and white shoes. $65.00.

Ken® in "The Yachtsman" #0789 - Denim slacks and jacket, red and white t-shirt, black shoes, white socks, white hat, and yachtsman book. $100.00.

Allen® in "Drum Major" #0775 - White jacket, red trousers, white plush hat, white socks and shoes, and baton. $80.00.

Ken® in "Special Date" #1401 - Navy suit, white long sleeve shirt, red tie, black shoes and socks. $70.00.

Ken® Doll in "Country Clubbin'" #1400 - Black and white check jacket, black slacks. Shirt, tie, shoes, and socks were not included in this set. $70.00.

Allen® Doll in "Ken Skin Diver" #1406 - Orange hooded sweat shirt, striped swim trunks, green fins, snorkel, and mask. $45.00.

Ken® Doll in "Boxer" (Pack) - Blue trunks, boxing gloves, black gym shoes. $35.00.

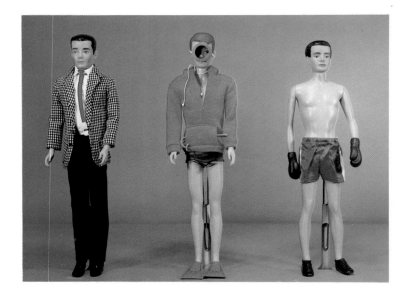

Ken® Doll in "Going Bowling" #1403 - Red shirt and gray slacks (shoes and socks not included). $40.00.

Allen® Doll in "Fraternity Meeting" #1408 - Brown slacks, white polo shirt, and brown and white cardigan (shoes and socks not included). $40.00.

Ken® Doll in "Goin Huntin' " #1409 - Red cap, red plaid shirt, blue jeans, and boots, plus hunting gun. $55.00.

Ken® Doll in "Cheerful Chef" Pack Set - Apron with forked hot-dog, spatula, spoon, chef's hat, red checked bandana, and mitt. $45.00.

Ken® Doll in "Mr. Astronaut" - Silver space suit, brown gloves, space helmet, brown boots, and the American flag. $175.00.

Allen® Doll in "Off to Bed" #1413 - White and blue knit pajamas, plush slippers, alarm clock, glass of milk, red telephone, and book. $75.00.

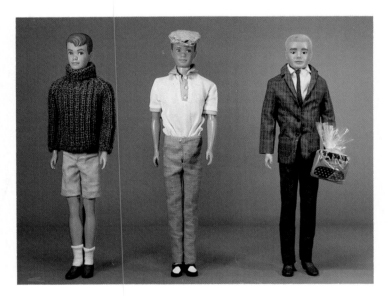

Allen® Doll in "Hiking Holiday" - Tan bermudas, green bulky sweater, brown shoes, and white socks. $60.00.

Allen® Doll in "Holiday" - Blue slacks, white knit shirt, white socks, black and white shoes. $70.00.

Ken® Doll in "College Student" #1416 - Brown slacks, green and brown plaid jacket, white shirt, brown tie, shoes and socks, typewriter. $75.00.

Allen® Doll in "Rovin' Reporter" #1417 - Navy blue slacks, red cardigan jacket, white shirt, black socks and shoes, and camera. $70.00.

Allen® Doll in "Best Man" #1425 - White dress jacket. black trousers, white dress shirt, red cumberbund and bow tie, black socks and shoes. $175.00.

Allen® Doll in "Jazz Concert" #1420 - Tan and blue short sleeve sweater, shirt, tan trousers, white socks, and white tennis shoes. $100.00.

103

Allen® Doll in "Seein' The Sights" #1421 - Red and navy tweed jacket, navy blue slacks, white long sleeve shirt, red tie, black shoes and socks. $100.00.

Ken® Doll in "Here Comes The Groom" #1426 - Gray dress coat (with tails), gray and white striped trousers, white high collar dress shirt, light gray vest, gray ascot tie, light gray suede gloves, black shoes and socks, and light gray top hat. Very rare. $275.00.

Ken® Doll in "T.V.'s Good Tonight" #1419 - Red monogrammed robe, red scuffs, and portable TV set. $75.00.

Ken® Doll in "Summer Job" #1422 - Gray jacket and trousers, moss green and white striped long sleeve shirt, moss green tie, black shoes and socks. Hard to find. $160.00.

Allen® Doll in "Ken A GO GO" #1423 - Red, gold, and green striped shirt, gold slacks, fake black fur wig, white socks, and tennis shoes, gold ukulele and strap, and microphone. $100.00.

Ken® Doll in "Time to Turn In" #1418 - Navy blue and red polka dot pajama and electric razor. $60.00.

Ken® Doll in "Business Appointment" #1424 - Black and white tweed overcoat, black felt hat, black leather type gloves, black brief case, and Mattel Daily News Paper, (suit not included), hardest of all Ken's outfits to find, very rare. $275.00.

Assorted Ken® Packs.
$20.00 to $25.00 each.

Ken® Doll returns after a two year sabbatical. He now talks and shows signs of maturing.

Ken® Doll in "Rally Gear" #1429 - Leatherette jacket, gold duck slacks, gold, orange, and blue striped shirt, brown high boots. $30.00.

Brad® Doll, Ken® Doll's new friend in "Town Turtle" #1430 - Turtle neck dickie, blue sport jacket, blue and gray bell bottom slacks, black loafers. $30.00.

Brad® Doll in "Groovy Formal" - Red Marou jacket, white long sleeve ascot shirt, gold and red brocade vest, white shoes. $35.00.

Ken® Doll in "Play It Cool" #1433 - Gold felt jacket, gold and black plaid slacks, red turtle-neck pullover, brown loafers. $40.00.

Ken® Doll in "Big Business" #1434 - Black and white check suit, turquoise shirt, striped pink tie, and black loafers. $40.00.

Ken® Doll in "Bold Gold" #1436 - Gold turtle-neck pullover, orange and gold plaid sport jacket, gold slacks, gold socks, and brown shoes. $40.00.

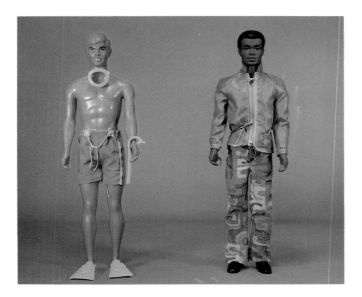

Ken® Doll and Brad® Doll in "Shore Lines" #1435 - (2 in 1 set) Ken in turquoise and gold swim trunks, face mask, snorkle and swim fins. Brad in turquoise zippered slicker jacket and multicolored slacks. (Shoes not included in set.) $50.00.

Not pictured. Ken® Doll's "Breakfast at 7" #1428 - Orange and gold robe and belt, gold and orange plaid pajamas, brown leather-type scuffs, and electic razor. $40.00.

Ken® Doll in "Sea Scene" #1449 - Red, white, and blue striped zippered jacket and slacks, blue turtle-neck dickie, white belt (not pictured). This set came with two different sets of shoes, white beach sandals, and white tennis shoes. $40.00.

Brad® Doll in "V.I.P. Scene" #1473 - Red and black plaid suit, red short sleeve shirt, white tie, black socks and shoes. $40.00.

Ken® Doll in "Casual Scene" #1472 - Blue felt short coat, blue and red knit slacks, white dickie, blue socks, and black shoes. $40.00.

Ken® Doll in "Ski-ing Scene" #1438 - Gold, red, and blue striped turtle-neck pullover ski sweater with matching ski cap, navy blue slacks, black shoes and socks, skis, and poles. $40.00.

Ken® Doll in "Suede Scene" #1439 - Suede trousers, red and gold print long sleeve shirt, gold socks and shoes. $40.00.

Ken® Doll in "Night Scene" #1496 - Wine colored velveteen dress jacket trimmed with satin, velveteen trousers, satin cumberbund, white ruffled front dickie with black bow tie, black socks and shoes. $45.00.

Malibu Ken® Gift Set - "Surf's In," This is the only gift set offered just for Ken. $275.00.

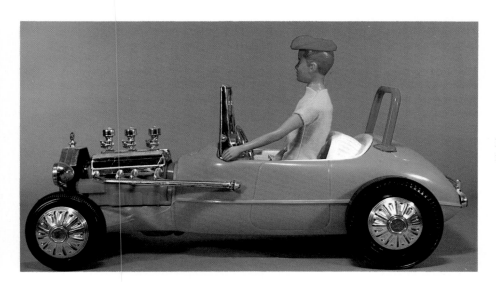

Ken's® "Hot Rod." Hard to find in fine condition. $150.00.

Ken's® Wardrobe Closet - Made by Suzie Goose, licensed by Mattel. $50.00.

Child-size vinyl and foam throw pillow. $35.00.

First Ken® case - 1961. Made in assorted colors. $20.00.

Second Ken® case - 1963. Made in assorted colors. $20.00.

Ken® and Allen® case. Sold only in France. $150.00.

Zeb Zachary - an experienced Indian Fighter comes with same field and battle acessories as Maddox and Custer. Hard to find. $70.00 M.I.B.

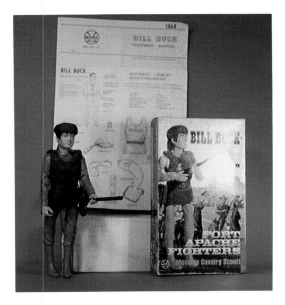

Scout Bill Buck equipped to live in the wild west with 13 pieces including coonskin cap and vest. Hard to find. $80.00 M.I.B.

Jed Gibson. Later and very hard to find. Black figure. $125.00 mint and complete.

Daniel Boone with coonskin cap and vest and same equipment as Bill Buck. This figure does not have moveable legs. Rare. $85.00 mint and complete.

Sheriff Garrett (Sheriff Goode in Canada) - protector of the West with 25 pieces of clothing, weapons, and utensils in silver and black. Rare. $80.00 M.I.B.

Princess Wild Flower is the most exciting collectible figure in the set. A true collector's item of Indian lore. She has 22 articles of clothing, jewelry, and cooking utensils, plus a baby and back carrier. $65.00 M.I.B.

Princess Wild Flower accessories and clothing. $60.00 mint and complete.

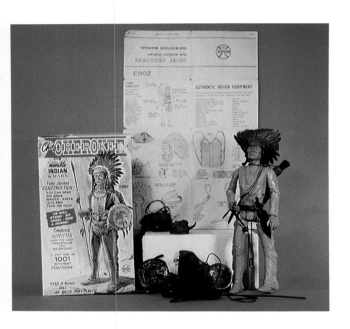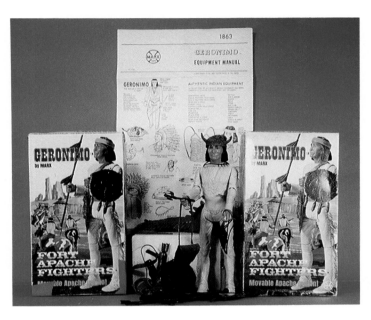

Chief Cherokee. Historically authenic with 37-piece accessory wardrobe. Fully documented. $55.00 M.I.B.

Fighting Geronimo - Leading Indian. $65.00 M.I.B. $50.00 mint and complete.

Geronimo and Cherokee in different color variarion accessories. $65.00 mint and complete.

Chief Cherokee color variation in accessories. A later version. $65.00 mint and complete.

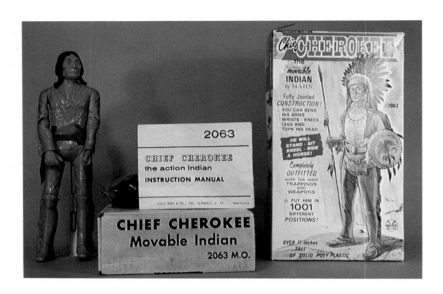

Chief Cherokee showing department store shipping box and regular photo box. $55.00 M.I.B.

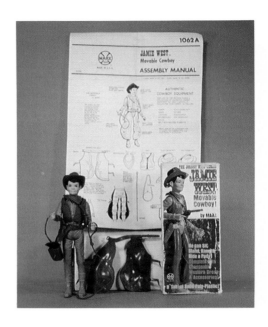

Jamie West has brown hair and is outfitted with the same 13 accessories as Jay. $50.00 M.I.B.

Fighting Eagle - Fierce Young Brave has same 37-piece accessories as Chief Cherokee. $65.00 M.I.B.

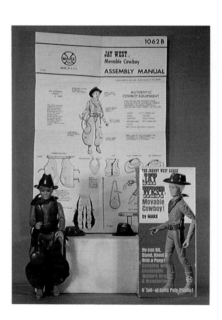

Jay West a blonde outfitted for range or ranch with 13 individual accessories. $45.00 M.I.B.

Jay West with brighter colored accessories. Later version. $40.00 mint and complete.

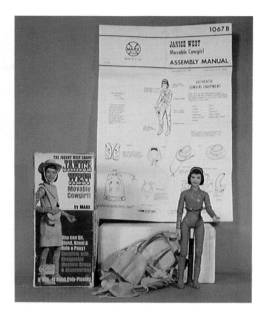

Janice West with brown hair, 9" tall, comes with 14-piece accessory set. $45.00 M.I.B.

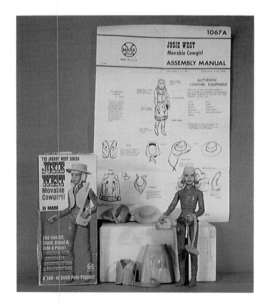

Josie West 9" figure with blonde side tails comes with the same 14-piece accessory set as Janice. $45.00 M.I.B.

Josie West in later color variation. $35.00 mint and complete.

Not Shown:
Storm Cloud Pinto, 14½" horse for any Indian figure with saddle-blanket and hackamore, spotted brown or black with white. $30.00 M.I.B.

Buckskin Horse, brown or Palomino coloring, with moving head, saddle, and 16 accessories, any 11½" figure can mount. $25.00 M.I.B.

Comanche Horse comes with 16 accessories including saddle, rich brown color. Completely moveable horse has 13 hinges. $30.00 M.I.B.

Thunderbolt Johnny West's Horse. 11½" moveable figure, available in Palomino, brown, or black each with saddle and 16 accessories. $30.00 M.I.B.

Thunderbolt, dark brown version. $25.00 mint and complete.

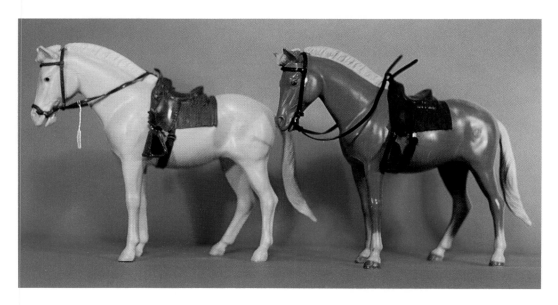

Pancho Horse, a 12½" long Welsh Pony with 9 accessories including saddle. Available in bay or brown color. Perfect for all West children. $25.00 mint and complete.

Buckboard and Horse. Fan hoof-wheeled horse pulls a 36" long rig. Authentic down to the springs. $65.00 M.I.B.

Covered Wagon and Horse. Waterproof canopy, 34" long, pulled by a hoof-wheeled brown horse. $70.00 M.I.B.

Johnny West Ranch Wagon. Trailer and Jeep. Picture missing windshiled and steering wheel. A very unusual item. Late issue. $75.00 mint and complete.

Steve Scout. $25.00 mint.
Bob Scout. $30.00 M.I.B.
Craig Cub Scout. $30.00 M.I.B.

Not Shown
Dave Cub Scout. $30.00 M.I.B.
Bill mail offer scout, near impossible to find. $45.00 mint and complete.

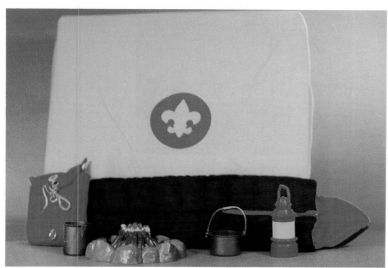

Camping Set: tent, sleeping bag, lantern, cooking, utensils, and campfire. $25.00 mint.

First Aid Equipment:

Stretcher. $5.00.
Crutches. $7.00 pair.
Oxygen Tank. $5.00.
Blinker Light. $7.00.

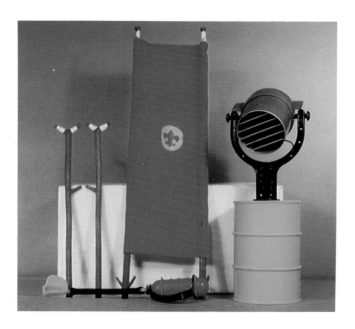

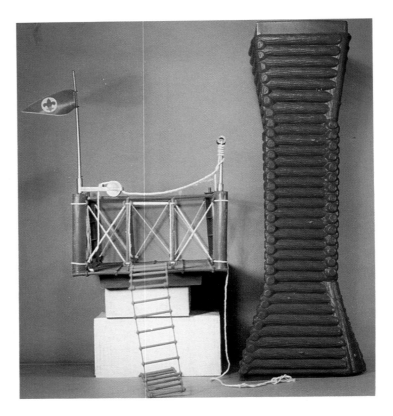

High Adventure Observation Tower, over 42" tall. $25.00 complete.

High Adventure Jeep with equipment and flag. $30.00.

Trailer and canoe. $25.00.

The Six Million Dollar Man

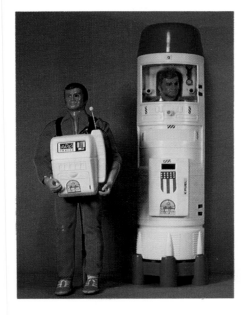

Steve Austin, The Bionic Man with radio pack. $20.00.

The Bionic Man. $25.00 M.I.B.

Capsule. $20.00.

Oscar Goldman's brief case. $30.00.

Oscar Goldman. $35.00 M.I.B.

Jamie Sommer, The Bionic Woman. $20.00 mint and complete. $25.00 M.I.B.

The Bionic Man Big Foot. $25.00.

The Bionic Woman Robot. $15.00.

The Bionic Man Adventure.

Test flight at 75,000 feet Set. $20.00 M.O.C.

The Bionic Man Adventure.

Under Cover Assignment Set. $20.00.

The Bionic Man Adventure.

Mission on Mars and Figure. $35.00.

Outfit only. $25.00 M.O.C.

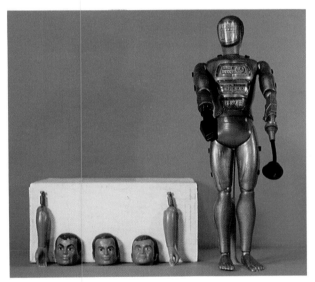

The Bionic Man Masketron Robot. $20.00.
Parts of this figure have the tendency to decompose
and melt. Difficult to find one in perfect condition.

The Bionic Woman Con-
vertable with ejecting seat
and many extras. $40.00.
$50.00 M.I.B.

The Bionic Woman Game
by Parker Brothers. $20.00.

BIG JIM

by Mattel

This doll is highly collectible, yet priced right for the beginner collector. There is a lot out there, vehicles, camping gear, and clothing. Big Jim was also produced in foreign countries and Canada. There are variations and some are not available in the U.S. He is vinyl and 9½" tall. He also has an extensive wardrobe.

Four unknown characters from the Big Jim Collection. $10.00 to 20.00 each.

Big Jim Argentina Gaucho. $12.00 M.I.B.

Big Jim Tennis. $12.00 M.I.B.

Big Jim Indian Chief. $12.00 M.I.B.

Big Jim Motorcross. $12.00 M.I.B.

Big Jim Camper and Accesories.
$40.00 mint and complete.

Big Jim Rescue Rig and accessories. $50.00 mint and complete.

Big Jim Sky Commander Jet opens up to 4½ ft. long with Communications Center cargo bay, doors (open), seat, map table, and bunk bed. $35.00 mint and complete.

Big Jim Adventure Case from Germany. $25.00 mint.

Big Jim Terror Off Tahiti, Deep Sea Diver Set. $20.00 mint and complete.

Big Jim Motorcross Honda. $20.00 mint and complete.

Big Jim Camping Tent. $18.00 mint and complete.

Big Jim Safari Hut. $25.00 mint.

Big Jim Safari Hut interior.

MISCELLANEOUS

This last chapter will include a little of this and a little of that. Most of these dolls have not been pictured in other books. They are considered interesting and collectible.

The Man From U.N.C.L.E.

This was a television show in the 1960's. The character figures were a product of Gilbert Toys, representing members of U.N.C.L.E. and Thrush, top secret organizations.

Napoleon Solo played by Robert Vaughn. $110.00 mint and complete.
Courtesy of Scott Mick.

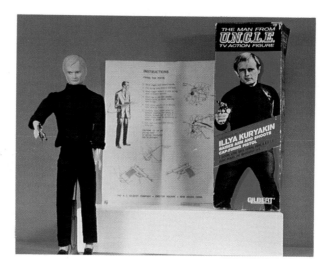

Illya Kuryakin played by David McCallum, same accessories as Solo. $110.00 M.I.B.
Courtesy of Scott Mick.

Illya Kuryakin in a different outfit. Outfit only $25.00 mint and complete.

The Man from U.N.C.L.E. extra accessories. Parachute and vest. $20.00 mint.

James Bond Secret Agent 007

James Bond 11" figure by Gilbert.
Figure in outfit sold separately. $85.00 mint and complete.

Game $45.00.

James Bond by Gilbert in Scuba Suit $60.00 complete.

James Bond Liston & Read record book *A View to Kill.* $15.00.

James Bond "Thunderball" game. $45.00.

Extra: Disguise Kit. $15.00.   The Jump Set. $15.00.

 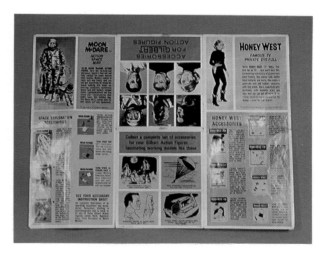

Colored information folder with description of famous show and TV character dolls by Gilbert. $10.00.

Dr. Ben Casey & Dr. Kildare

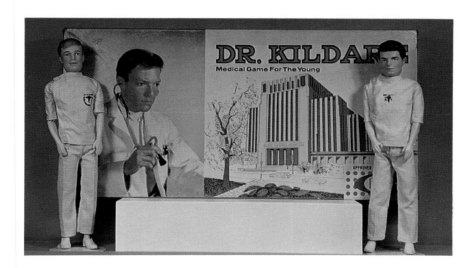

Dr. Ben Casey was played by Vince Edwards. Dr. Kildare was played by Richard Chamberlain. These figures are unmarked. Maker unknown.

Dr. Ben Casey. $75.00.   Dr. Kildare. $100.00.
Courtesy of Scott Mick

The Lone Ranger

The Lone Ranger by Gabriel. Pictured from left to right:

Butch Cavendish on Smoke. $45.00.   Red Sleeves. Very rare. $50.00.

Tonto on Scout. $50.00.   Lone Ranger on Silver. $50.00.

Little Bear. Very rare. $50.00.   Dan Reed on Banjo. Hard to find. $45.00.

This was a Woolworth Woolco Display. Complete Display $500.00.

The Lone Ranger by Gabriel.

Tribal Teepee. $25.00 M.I.B.   Prairie Wagon. $40.00 M.I.B.

Action Jackson by Mego

Black Dinah-Mite and Action Jackson by Mego. Black Dinah-Mite Hard to find. $20.00 M.I.B.

Action Jackson. $15.00 M.I.B.
Action Jackson shown with outfit sold separately.

Dinah-Mite. Display package with doll and four outfits. $55.00.

Dinah-Mite Doll. $20.00 M.I.B.

Dinah-Mite paper dolls, uncut. $8.00.

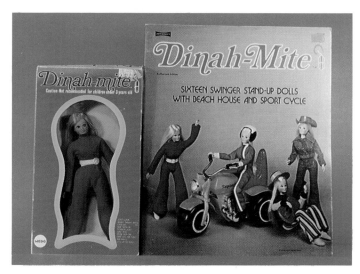

Lassie and Friends

Lassie and her Friends by Gabriel. Fully jointed figures. $95.00.

Also available: Lassie's Farm Play Set. Not shown $50.00.

Heroes of the American Revolution

There were seven 8" plastic figures in this set issued in the 1980's. Each doll was packaged in a box with the history of the represented character.

Top: George Washington. $10.00 M.I.B.

Left to Right: John Paul Jones. $10.00 M.I.B.   Paul Revere. $10.00 M.I.B.

Thomas Jeferson. $10.00 M.I.B.   Nathan Hale. $10.00 M.I.B.

Not pictured: Patrick Henry. $10.00 M.I.B.   Benjamin Franklin. $10.00 M.I.B.

Bible Greats

A quite interesting and also educational collectable item. Found in religious stores. Shows body structure.

Goliath. $25.00 M.I.B.

Jonah and the whale. $35.00 M.I.B.

Daniel and the lion. $35.00 M.I.B.

The stories of Joseph. $15.00 M.I.P.

Samson. $15.00 M.I.P.

The stories of Deborah. $15.00 M.I.P.

Ruth. $15.00 M.I.P.

Archie and Friends

The first Archie and Friends figures were a product of Marx Toys. They were later made by other manufacturers.

Archie. $30.00 M.I.P.   Jughead. $30.00 M.I.P.

Veronica. $30.00 M.I.P.   Betty. $30.00 M.I.P.

Vinyl Bendies.

Veronica. $20.00 M.I.P.   Archie. $20.00 M.I.P.

Jughead. $20.00 M.I.P.   Betty (not shown). $20.00 M.I.P.

Cloth stuffed. These dolls are rarely found.

Jughead. $25.00 M.I.P.   Archie. $25.00 M.I.P.

Betty. $25.00 M.I.P.   Veronica. $25.00. M.I.P.

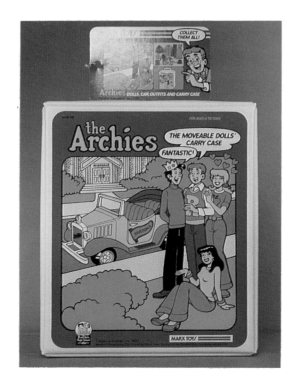

Archie Doll and accessory case. $25.00.

The Archie Jalopy. A rare and very difficult item to find. $50.00 and up M.I.B.

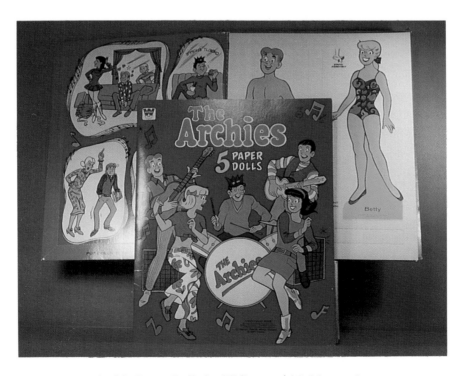

Archie Paper Dolls by Whitman. $10.00 uncut.

There was an assortment of extra clothing for Archie and Friends. $6.00 each M.I.P.

Fast Food Items.

Set of 6. $30.00.
$4.00 each.

Archie Head hand stand puppet. $15.00.   Archie pinback button. $15.00.

Archie kaleidoscope. 48.00.   Archie View-Master set. $15.00.

Archie trading cards given as a Halloween treat. $6.00 each.

ABOUT THE AUTHORS

Due to their love of dolls, Paris and Susan felt the urge to share their knowledge with others:

Paris: through photography

Susan: through research and play.

They have authored six books to date. The authors continue to promote six doll shows yearly, and attend other doll shows and collectors' conventions.

Paris and Susan do not pretend to be experts. They just like sharing information with other enthusiasts.

They hope their books have brought pleasure to everyone and will continue to do so in the future.

DOLLS, FIGURES & TEDDY BEARS

2382	Advertising Dolls, Identification & Values, Robison & Sellers	$9.95
2079	Barbie Doll Fashions, Volume I, Eames	$24.95
3957	Barbie Exclusives, Rana	$18.95
4557	Barbie, The First 30 Years, Deutsch	$24.95
3310	Black Dolls, 1820–1991, Perkins	$17.95
3873	Black Dolls, Book II, Perkins	$17.95
3810	Chatty Cathy Dolls, Lewis	$15.95
4559	Collectible Action Figures, Manos	$17.95
1529	Collector's Encyclopedia of Barbie Dolls, DeWein	$19.95
4506	Collector's Guide to Dolls in Uniform, Bourgeois	$18.95
3727	Collector's Guide to Ideal Dolls, Izen	$18.95
3728	Collector's Guide to Miniature Teddy Bears, Powell	$17.95
3967	Collector's Guide to Trolls, Peterson	$19.95
3971	Madame Alexander Dolls Price Guide #20, Smith	$9.95
2186	Modern Collector's Dolls II, Smith	$17.95
2187	Modern Collector's Dolls III, Smith	$17.95
2188	Modern Collector's Dolls IV, Smith	$17.95
2189	Modern Collector's Dolls V, Smith	$17.95
3733	Modern Collector's Dolls, Sixth Series, Smith	$24.95
3991	Modern Collector's Dolls, Seventh Series, Smith	$24.95
4472	Modern Collector's Dolls Update, Smith	$9.95
1972	Patricia Smith's Doll Values, Antique to Modern, 11th Edition	$12.95
4826	Story of Barbie, Westenhouser	$19.95
1513	Teddy Bears & Steiff Animals, Mandel	$9.95
1817	Teddy Bears & Steiff Animals, 2nd Series, Mandel	$19.95
2084	Teddy Bears, Annalee's & Steiff Animals, 3rd Series, Mandel	$19.95
1808	Wonder of Barbie, Manos	$9.95
1430	World of Barbie Dolls, Manos	$9.95

TOYS, MARBLES & CHRISTMAS COLLECTIBLES

3427	Advertising Character Collectibles, Dotz	$17.95
2333	Antique & Collector's Marbles, 3rd Ed., Grist	$9.95
3827	Antique & Collector's Toys, 1870–1950, Longest	$24.95
3956	Baby Boomer Games, Identification & Value Guide, Polizzi	$24.95
3514	Character Toys & Collectibles, Longest	$19.95
3750	Character Toys & Collector's, 2nd Series, Longest	$19.95
4717	Christmas Collectibles, 2nd Edition, Whitmyer	$24.95
4752	Christmas Ornaments, Lights & Decorations, Johnson	$19.95
1874	Collectible Coca-Cola Toy Trucks, deCourtivron	$24.95
3338	Collector's Encyclopedia of Disneyana, Longest, Stern	$24.95
1566	Collector's Guide to Tootsietoys, 2nd Ed Richter	$19.95
3436	Grist's Big Book of Marbles	$19.95
3970	Grist's Machine-Made & Contemporary Marbles, 2nd Ed.	$9.95
4732	Matchbox® Toys, 1948 to 1993, Johnson	$18.95
3823	Mego Toys, An Illustrated Value Guide, Chrouch	15.95
1540	Modern Toys 1930–1980, Baker	$19.95
3888	Motorcycle Toys, Antique & Contemporary, Gentry/Downs	$18.95
3954	Schroeder's Collectible Toys, Antique to Modern Price Guide, 2nd Ed	$17.95
1886	Stern's Guide to Disney Collectibles	$14.95
2139	Stern's Guide to Disney Collectibles, 2nd Series	$14.95
3975	Stern's Guide to Disney Collectibles, 3rd Series	$18.95
2028	Toys, Antique & Collectible, Longest	$14.95
3974	Zany Characters of the Ad World, Lamphier	$16.95

JEWELRY, HATPINS, WATCHES & PURSES

1712	Antique & Collector's Thimbles & Accessories, Mathis	$19.95
1748	Antique Purses, Revised Second Ed., Holiner	$19.95
1278	Art Nouveau & Art Deco Jewelry, Baker	$9.95
3875	Collecting Antique Stickpins, Kerins	$16.95
3722	Collector's Ency. of Compacts, Carryalls & Face Powder Boxes, Mueller	$24.95
3992	Complete Price Guide to Watches, #15, Shugart	$21.95
4716	Fifty Years of Collectible Fashion Jewelry, 1925-1975, Baker	$19.95
1424	Hatpins & Hatpin Holders, Baker	$9.95
1181	100 Years of Collectible Jewelry, 1850-1950, Baker	$9.95
4348	20th Century Fashionable Plastic Jewelry, Baker	$19.95
1830	Vintage Vanity Bags & Purses, Gerson	$24.95

FURNITURE

1457	American Oak Furniture, McNerney	$9.95
3716	American Oak Furniture, Book II, McNerney	$12.95
1118	Antique Oak Furniture, Hill	$7.95
3832	Collector's Encyclopedia of American Furniture, Vol. I, Swedberg	$24.95
3271	Collector's Encyclopedia of American Furniture, Vol. II, Swedberg	$24.95
3720	Collector's Encyclopedia of American Furniture, Vol. III, Swedberg	$24.95
1437	Collector's Guide to Country Furniture, Raycraft	$9.95
3878	Collector's Guide to Oak Furniture, George	$12.95
1755	Furniture of the Depression Era, Swedberg	$19.95
3906	Heywood-Wakefield Modern Furniture, Rouland	$18.95
1965	Pine Furniture, Our American Heritage, McNerney	$14.95
1885	Victorian Furniture, Our American Heritage, McNerney	$9.95
3829	Victorian Furniture, Our American Heritage, Book II, McNerney	$9.95
3869	Victorian Furniture books, 2 volume set, McNerney	$19.90

INDIANS, GUNS, KNIVES, TOOLS, PRIMITIVES

1868	Antique Tools, Our American Heritage, McNerney	$9.95
2015	Archaic Indian Points & Knives, Edler	$14.95
1426	Arrowheads & Projectile Points, Hothem	$7.95
2279	Indian Artifacts of the Midwest, Hothem	$14.95
3885	Indian Artifacts of the Midwest, Book II, Hothem	$16.95
1964	Indian Axes & Related Stone Artifacts, Hothem	$14.95
2023	Keen Kutter Collectibles, Heuring	$14.95
3887	Modern Guns, Identification & Values, 10th Ed., Quertermous	$12.95
2164	Primitives, Our American Heritage, McNerney	$9.95
1759	Primitives, Our American Heritage, Series II, McNerney	$14.95
3325	Standard Knife Collector's Guide, 2nd Ed., Ritchie & Stewart	$12.95

PAPER COLLECTIBLES & BOOKS

1441	Collector's Guide to Post Cards, Wood	$9.95
2081	Guide to Collecting Cookbooks, Allen	$14.95
3969	Huxford's Old Book Value Guide, 7th Ed.	$19.95
3821	Huxford's Paperback Value Guide	$19.95
2080	Price Guide to Cookbooks & Recipe Leaflets, Dickinson	$9.95
3973	Sheet Music Reference & Price Guide, 2nd Ed., Pafik & Guiheen	$19.95

OTHER COLLECTIBLES

2280	Advertising Playing Cards, Grist	$16.95
2269	Antique Brass & Copper Collectibles, Gaston	$16.95
1880	Antique Iron, McNerney	$9.95
3872	Antique Tins, Dodge	$24.95
1714	Black Collectibles, Gibbs	$19.95
1128	Bottle Pricing Guide, 3rd Ed., Cleveland	$7.95
3959	Cereal Box Bonanza, The 1950's, Bruce	$19.95
3718	Collector's Aluminum, Grist	$16.95
4560	Collectible Cats, An Identification & Value Guide, Book II, Fyke	$19.95
1634	Collector's Ency. of Figural & Novelty Salt & Pepper Shakers, Davern	$19.95
2020	Collector's Ency. of Figural & Novelty Salt & Pepper Shakers, Vol. II, Davern	$19.95
2018	Collector's Encyclopedia of Granite Ware, Greguire	$24.95
3430	Collector's Encyclopedia of Granite Ware, Book II, Greguire	$24.95
3879	Collector's Guide to Antique Radios, 3rd Ed., Bunis	$18.95
1916	Collector's Guide to Art Deco, Gaston	$14.95
3880	Collector's Guide to Cigarette Lighters, Flanagan	$17.95
1537	Collector's Guide to Country Baskets, Raycraft	$9.95
3966	Collector's Guide to Inkwells, Identification & Values, Badders	$18.95
3881	Collector's Guide to Novelty Radios, Bunis/Breed	$18.95
3729	Collector's Guide to Snow Domes, Guarnaccia	$18.95
3730	Collector's Guide to Transistor Radios, Bunis	$15.95
2276	Decoys, Kangas	$24.95
1629	Doorstops, Identification & Values, Bertoia	$9.95
3968	Fishing Lure Collectibles, Murphy/Edmisten	$24.95
4568	Flea Market Trader, 10th Ed., Huxford	$12.95
3819	General Store Collectibles, Wilson	$24.95
2215	Goldstein's Coca-Cola Collectibles	$16.95
3884	Huxford's Collector's Advertising, 2nd Ed.	$24.95
2216	Kitchen Antiques, 1790–1940, McNerney	$14.95
1782	1,000 Fruit Jars, 5th Edition, Schroeder	$5.95
3321	Ornamental & Figural Nutcrackers, Rittenhouse	$16.95
2026	Railroad Collectibles, 4th Ed., Baker	$14.95
1632	Salt & Pepper Shakers, Guarnaccia	$9.95
1888	Salt & Pepper Shakers II, Identification & Value Guide, Book II, Guarnaccia	$14.95
2220	Salt & Pepper Shakers III, Guarnaccia	$14.95
3443	Salt & Pepper Shakers IV, Guarnaccia	$18.95
2096	Silverplated Flatware, Revised 4th Edition, Hagan	$14.95
1922	Standard Old Bottle Price Guide, Sellari	$14.95
3892	Toy & Miniature Sewing Machines, Thomas	$18.95
3828	Value Guide to Advertising Memorabilia, Summers	$18.95
3977	Value Guide to Gas Station Memorabilia	$24.95
3978	Wanted to Buy, 5th Edition	$9.95

This is only a partial listing of the books on collectibles that are available from Collector Books. All books are well illustrated and contain current values. Most of our books are available from your local bookseller, antique dealer, or public library. If you are unable to locate certain titles in your area, you may order by mail from COLLECTOR BOOKS, P.O. Box 3009, Paducah, KY 42002-3009. Customers with Visa or MasterCard may phone in orders from 7:00–5:00 CST, Monday–Friday, Toll Free 1-800-626-5420. Add $2.00 for postage for the first book ordered and $0.30 for each additional book. Include item number, title, and price when ordering. Allow 14 to 21 days for delivery.

Schroeder's ANTIQUES Price Guide

. . . is the #1 best-selling antiques & collectibles value guide on the market today, and here's why . . .

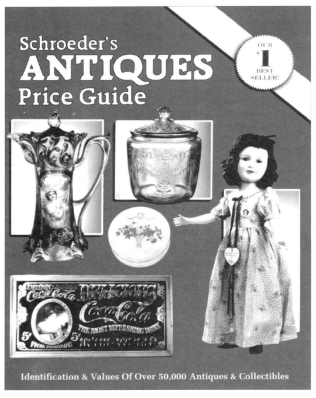

8½ x 11, 608 Pages, $12.95

• More than 300 advisors, well-known dealers, and top-notch collectors work together with our editors to bring you accurate information regarding pricing and identification.

• More than 45,000 items in almost 500 categories are listed along with hundreds of sharp original photos that illustrate not only the rare and unusual, but the common, popular collectibles as well.

• Each large close-up shot shows important details clearly. Every subject is represented with histories and background information, a feature not found in any of our competitors' publications.

• Our editors keep abreast of newly developing trends, often adding several new categories a year as the need arises.

If it merits the interest of today's collector, you'll find it in *Schroeder's*. And you can feel confident that the information we publish is up to date and accurate. Our advisors thoroughly check each category to spot inconsistencies, listings that may not be entirely reflective of market dealings, and lines too vague to be of merit. Only the best of the lot remains for publication.

Without doubt, you'll find
SCHROEDER'S ANTIQUES PRICE GUIDE
the only one to buy for
reliable information and values.

COLLECTOR BOOKS
A Division of Schroeder Publishing Co., Inc.